ENGLAND'S EDGING

Part Two

2021

Publishing without ...

EDAY

KW17 2AB: August 1987

Welcome to Scotland   that hint of old North
Riding   from the Cortina   Then we grasped
their silver wedding   forty years ago
like a malt with water   beck under brae
Lowlands   Yorkshire   Once   in our first drive north
we watched an old and younger   couple   scold
our nerve as we took to Scotland   The end
of that island was English   commandeered
The Pub   The Garden   Do as they do not
and Orcadian fields   lay lower   paused.

RHODES AIRPORT

GR85 106: 18/9/2019

*Turn off your mobile device or switch now
to flight mode*   But from his cordon of half-
drawn pleats   Thomas has cooked a call   We smile
but live out now   what that steward knew then
that planes would fall from the sky   liveries
ditched like unpaid armies   At hording gates
the masses queue like migrants   cases packed
with what would once return them   And tablets
buzz with half-dissected truths   as we trust
towards the void   above   below   ahead.

NANOU

AE6 8AN

That yacht's too big   for this furrow of bay
but it sends us back   to tamarisk shade
where parasols frown   The freight weighs anchor
against some myth of Greece   we'd thought we knew
A proboscis slides to port   jet skis flirt
with over-board folk   and party strains shoot
up the rubbled woods   The tavern-lads buzz
through naps and waves   but fail to wake the peace
Their Dad retrieves a shotgun   cracks barrels
up each shore   and the plump hull blinks   and leaves.

GRAYS

RM20 3FH: 23/10/2019

They've really done it now   I made to rant
as the online-off-beam fragment of junk
we didn't need   fell back to whim and scrapped
itself in tracking   A small obstructive
unpaid balance   and many vans like these
play blind and lose their loads   while in our no-
-man's-planned arrival hells   you can nearly
hear those last reports of life   the bolted
shout and strangled gasp   or air brakes letting
someone chill   while a shipment hits the sack.

THE GRAND ARCADE

CB2 3NB

They ejected one precinct   and charged it
with robbing the weekend hordes   of their right
affray   through the fissures of breeze blockades
In stripped-out light   it became an index
as vacant as   an unmapped underpass
Now the basilica's brass is calling
as if incense could swing   below those domes
He bolted from Superdrug   homelessly
soon   then the squad arrived and stuck him fast
to the sacred tiles   And out came the phones.

SYMI HARBOUR

GR85 600

Life on the ledge of Europe   Those dicey
homes roll up the fruitless hills   their shutters
shut like eyes   letting the ferries suggest
that classical catch of the Greece we want
all this to be   the workaday locals
making it easy   at our deck and call
Notice the police station terrace   hiding
three floors full of sleeping bag recliners
the gathering wave from Turkey   that looks
to see and wait and wonder   about home.

COWLEY ROAD

OX4 1XG: 2-12/12/19

Before you left this life   had you foreseen
the crowd who'd watch you lifted   so many
some flopped by the font?   Your life's recital
packed the aisles   like songs by all the ages
you'd retrieved   or lyrics taped with wonder
at how you knew what mattered   On that side
of the Cherwell the street lads   were half way
to bantering where they'd sleep   while placards
shouted choice or compromise   Ten days on
we go to vote   with you keeping an eye.

WHALLEY WEIR

BB7 9SR: December 2019

The water passed me fresh as winter air
blowing through beech woods on the Nab   where calls
from wren to buzzard   let December free
to float or flit   in a scrap of summer
I re-dream the day as the pub plays late
The Abbey's unsacked   and the country shop's
booted its broguers and tweed   to Blackburn
while niblicks dig allotments   on the greens
I'll go out early   and peel off the signs
Vote For   another who's chucked us down stream.

PLATFORM 5

CW2 6HR: 13/12/19

We are late into Crewe   the franchise find-
ing its way up the British aisles   in stripped
unvirginal uniform   and staring
out at the arable lakes   Here might be
either blue or red   but looks like somewhere
wet and mislaid   Three London lags clutch cards
near a pair of foghorns   fingers twiddle
and readers crouch   No one names how fate a-
lighted at these stops   this thirteenth Friday
My Kurdish cab-man said   *We lost*   *Drive on*.

BLACKPOOL NORTH PIER

FY1 1RA: 17/12/19

It ends with the starling particulates
and gusts up the isthmus   that iron a way
over tides and jetsam   We're tramlined down
dunes and breaking water   walking back south
past backstage neighbourhoods   upstaged by bit-
part snipe and oyster-catchers   frittering
But where the sea defences dip   we see
the shut up theatre of the town   the tyres
that fill the lido   then the spray against
the BnBs   and pillared paint-scuffed booths.

DISRAELI'S STATUE

L39 2AL: 3/1/2020

I've lost a pound or two   but the fresh year's
fortune might improve   if everyone took
a new look at themselves   and figured out
how to re-dress these ghosts of M & S
or H & M   or B & M   That bleached
kagoule who voted in   this oddball tribe
slides aside to pass the mum who   disowned
her dad for Wanting Out   The uni-hound
in shorts has seen   the green   and waves towards
the bloke who snubbed the lights   then flings the Vs.

NESSEBAR

BG82 30NE: 17/1/2020

Two weeks before we leave the lot   I find
behind a leather binding   sheaves of lei
and lev you'd kept   for a final Black Sea
mission   I file them with a piece to friends
that tells how age would stay   your helping hand
One note has the regime's hammer   above
some wheezing stacks   but on their strand we found
that locals talked in English   learnt from films
and worked and saved   towards the western dream
that islanders like us   are primed to leave.

WOLUWE-SAINT-PIERRE

BX1 1SO: January 2020

A tram delivers us   and outskirts draw
their drapes   as we're re-treading forty years
up the chestnut rails   and cherry rat runs
Less English here   we walk through the quarter
that trained us for thirteen years   in exile-
patois   or Belgian codes   and mulchy shades
of Europe   The house ignores our family
gaggle   as if it waits for some sudden
whitewash   or more space to park   or an eye
to sculpt the garden   That sorts the sortie.

FOLKESTONE'S WHITE HORSE

CT19 4QL

The carriage ceiling flaunts   our plunging speed
in sundering from home   below the sea
and France breaks dawn in arcing shafts   that spot
each urgent stab at breaking   in or out
And forty odd years later   level fields
look as kind and fresh and close   Light removes
from train to skyline   over whey farm walls
and clay roofs   furrow hollows   poplar pens
or mud canals   On one lane there's a pup
of the dog of a bitch   that saw us then.

COLL

PA78 6TA

This island wind-up   knocks at the key stones
of our houses   teases the trees with gusts
until a few are lent on steeply   heave
in leaf   screech and stumble   Two days later
next next door   spare their clumped leylandii
another gale   with a sawdust storm   Worlds
without woodland   thrived   through northern squalls   broke
my cover with views   onto breakers   gulls
boats rolled by heather-weather   There we watched
the English plunge   from Hebridean piers.

THE BRIDGEWATER HALL, MANCHESTER

M2 3WS: 14/3/2020

King C sang from Scotland With Love   his Fife
collective snared and well strung up   as night
became its own mutation   spreading through
the Hall   We were quarantined   back to left
front to right   in a show of no shows   set
by the set   to super-spread songs   to no
one   The merchandise   half pints at half time
and door-clan   held on   and after encores
Manchester held up   beyond our headlights
infecting   the shutters   pulled down like masks.

LEIGH

WA3 1AF: 28/3/2020

My getaway far skulked home   at five days

in   or wherever that ends as a part

of the final sum   Quarantined tarmac

re-ran the 62 milestones   turbine

trunks   reservoirs   Saddleworth   that flotsam-

jammed farm in the slipstream   The East Lancs. reached

like a rail   to slide return   at the cleft

of home   As I passed the green   a metal

flash of delivery van   out-paced the red

banked left   and spun up   like a child-chucked toy.

LADY'S WALK

L40 6HX: 10/4/2020

I stalk the wrong Good Friday   see a film
without a soundtrack   read a book that lies
remaindered   feel the sun's contagious threat
and know we need to scourge   these scrubby fields
and drag those stuck up lark-lads   down to earth
Let's get the honey hedge unsuckled   blow
this porcelained sky   back to the rain where
we walked   in the cancelled 2020
Better to jilt the cherry-debris   lock
the garden out   and board up the windows.

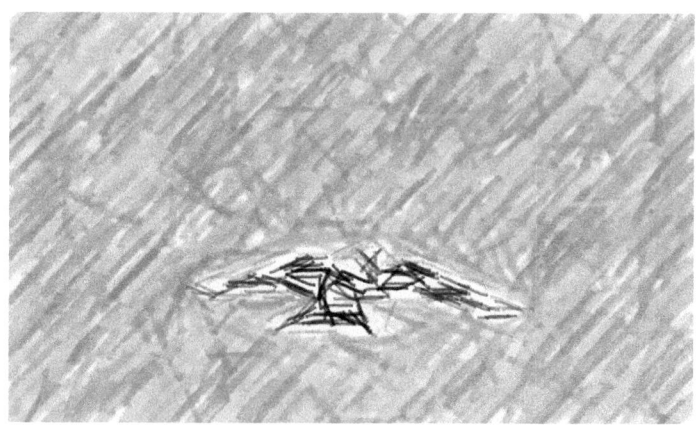

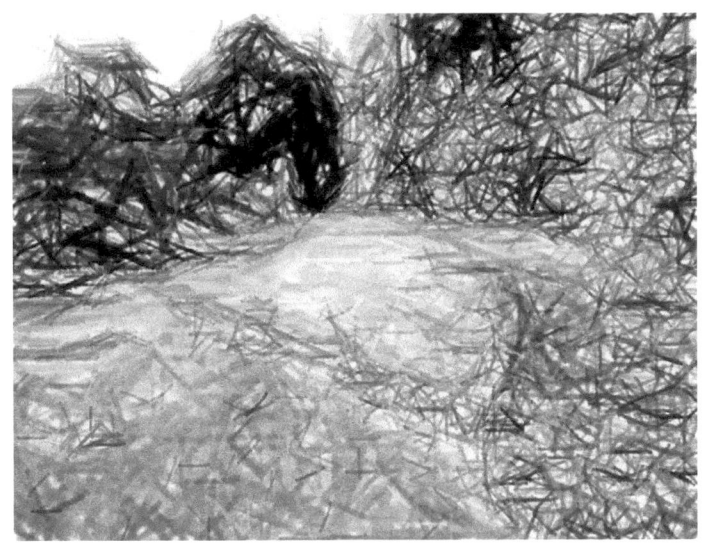

HETTINGA HOUSE

L40 5TR: 22/4/2020

The hospice slipped away   if God knows when
with a battle bravely bought   from builders
clerks they'd bribed   and those in-out darkening
drives   By the end   fewer nearest dears   would park
on the threshold   come with wreaths   Time would lend
no right relief   from all the viral wrongs
and nothing bothered anyone   as lives
cleared out   cleaned up   re-shaped   the death encased
in rhododendron   sycamore   red beech
dandelion   brick   and an unlocked gate.

SOUTH CAMBS.

5/5/2020

The garden walked   the tail waved   and always
a dog's life's lived to the fall   And so their
leaving catches us   as if surprised   Peg
and Tigger   Barney   Jackson   Zoe   Leah
Bruce and Rustler   Tango   Marble   one wraith
pack of remaindered names   we gave our dogs
Death shadowed each   through their pack of summers
and when we think of how they came   or left
these kennelled days   become much emptier
for canine constants   who can't walk us home.

TORSHAVN

FA4 80E: 12/5/2020

The park has trapped new prey   at the lounge bar
end   and we take a swerve   to miss a dose
of those aromas   toecaps   and anti-
social distance   Pubs have flung us out here
drunk   undrunk   withdrawn from isolation
tinnies in the bag   like long-gone lockdowns
Faroe's annual stream of sots   when the crowd
went home   those empties on a Narvik bench
the bus we joined in the Malá Fatra
fifty lags consumed by ale   off the piste.

ORMSKIRK STATION

L39 2YN: 15/5/2020

Five cars and the grunt of a bus that's wedged
have filled the only bays   and wait for one
or fewer grafters   brave enough to find
the line to Preston   Before we ailed   trees
were levelled   weed-banks chamfered   to link up
and light   bus and train   But the path's too cramped
to unfence now   Back on the nettle tracks
gnats like filaments plague the sun   and dogs
as frail as kittens   yowl   dangle from leads
and a pair of thrushes slip up a beech.

HODDESDON, HERTS.

EN11 8BJ: VE Day 2020

Coins in a coffee tin   emptied Mum's youth
across our lockdown   her father's Chinese
barrack days   Malayan change   Nazi francs
from 43   **Travail·Famille·Patrie**
or some tiny øre   branded with their cross
Mum found Europe mending through the 50s
stored a clutch of pfennig   several guilders
and masses of down-light lire   Now locked
requirement homes are blitzed   and we're to watch
as children of the War   re-live the fear.

LE CHAUMONT, SWISS JURA

GR0 3RE: 13/6/2020

Left in the barn   and clueless   rope in hand
I watched the calf   large eyes on me   weeks on
from his mother's cowshed vigil   lowing
lonely   and enticed him from the straw cell
of his life   to thistle meadows   under
sun   and played him out and off   to hay-high
capers   youth untethered   In English squares
they're trying to quell the bolting crowds   un-
bolted   freed from   deadlocked homes and history
calling us to rank   these rank infections.

CHRISTIE MILLER ROAD, SALISBURY

SP2 7EN: 18/6/2020

Driving to work   I'd pass that imagined
close   where three decades on   47
would toxify   rushing off its owners
One summer I dithered on a downland
rim   then ran from the rain   as Chernobyl
churned out terror vapours   hours away   Now
the telly re-tells these   as they weren't   not
like the now we know   from breathing   fretting
virally   A Scandi noir showed rabid
empty kennels   these   and other warnings.

ST. HELENS

WA10 4QH: 19/6/2020

Good luck to my workmates   still at your desk
or wherever you fetched up   lost or binned
in the final clearance   that whistle   black
and Fox by name   or the hi-viz wardrobe
splayed-out brolleys   binos   and that metal-
seeking wand that lit on fag foils   further
back   the hush hush toothbrush   splintered mirror
and backup poppy   so much to recall
from the ledger   shredded   best kept at home
as now we wonder   where the kids have gone.

TARLETON AND BEYOND

PR4 6RR: 28/6/2020
After Susan Hodgkins

Your art's from a northern palette   angled
sharp as a moss horizon   sure and true
like Becconsall's church   in the fields   its craft
as rare as the shrapnelled graves   In grafting
up there   pen and water   ink or pigment
sculpting gouge   lend themselves   to landscape   light
and every rushed stroke of living   leading
eye and insight   past that modest English
cusp   its landlocked Shore Road   pontoon moorings
pastures filling with sheep   and Ribble tides.

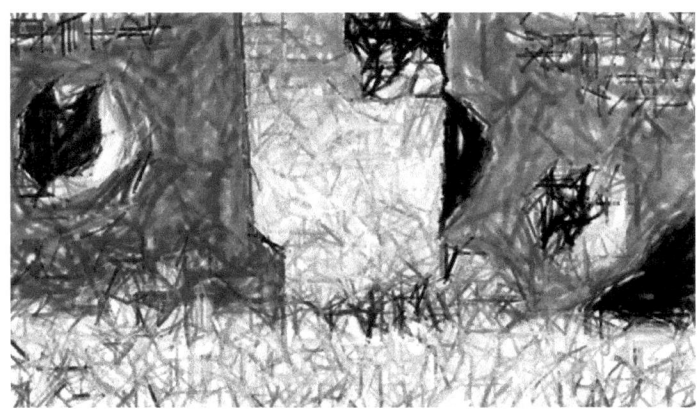

Fathers' Day, 2020

In the shame of the fathers the sons and ...
Our fathers   who are in limbo   hallo
if but by name   your moments came   your place
was filled   in homes that were your homes   Forgive
those who judge you as all the same   Forgo
them   your treasure trove   as we forget all
the treatment that others have blamed you for
Let's not be tempted to heap the evil
of the kingdom   its power and its story
upon them forever   or sigh   *Our men.*

FORBURY GARDENS, READING

RG1 3EU: 20/6/2020

Would Oscar say   we're hurt by those we'd like
to love?   As he watched death and the tent-shaped
sky   could he see the Abbey's gravelled paths
where we snapped a student prank?   Did we know
how love would tear apart   the best of us
one night in Jubilee gardens   forty
years before   that spectre   of envy   lust
and lovelessness   picked off three   happy lads
being glad   in that prism   of unlocked love
lost in Reading's quicklime?   Like yesterday.

M6: SHAP SUMMIT

CA10 3LQ: July 2020

Finding its wheels   the country   filled its roads
from the inside   edgewards   stocked up its boots
with the mothballed months   set sat-navs whittling
down the miles   unwinding   hand-gelled key codes
unbugged worktops   drafts to discharge   floor plans
and decking for distance   At Tebay   brakes
blink red ahead   we join them   at twenty
bike racks   lolling dogs   windows sliding down
then up   one lane of blocked exhausts   the slick
of carriageway   re-sheened   coned off   unmanned.

GOLDEN GROVE, WHITBY

YO22 5HH: August 2020

Márgarét   were you once a walker here   sprung
by your Uncle Gerard   father Arthur
from wicker gluts of herring   and bristled
masts?   Would you ghost that brined-up scenery
sometimes in summer   track the Esk up dreams
to Rigg Mill Beck?   Its cobbled verge and clefts
ghost a cascade   then walk the hamlet   back
to Whitby   Picture your last day   wanwood
at August's end   grieving how trees unleaf
from a hundred and forty falls ago.

STAITHES

TS13 5BQ: August 2020

They tooted from the brink   two British cars
jammed on the cobbled chute   split but defined
by its spats   of creel house and cottage kitsch
A deranged rover loading up   weekend
spoils   shriek by growl   to a macro-mini
slowdown locals   vocal showdown   The rest
became more English   momentary   hushed up
slate and inert   We thought we'd track the tide
how long we'd parked   or queue for some coffees
from a booth   then cower in plastic chairs.

COALPIT LANE, LATHOM

WN8 8UT

What's buried in these meadows and lane-wide
birch   and bramble ridges?   Throughout one war
horses pitched up from treks or trucks   shuddered
down trench-bound backwood ramps   and several miles
of narrow gauge   unloaded and broken
through Lathom's gardens   then sorted and hoofed
and shipped   over sea   to haul and falter
blast and fall   The line's lasting bones arise
through hawthorn and fence posts   on Firswood Road
past a stable-sized hut   off Engine Lane.

MERE BROW

PR4 6JR

The poplar walls and runnels   mark out farms
unfussed by spot lit   in out   gates   and spared
the Merx and SUVs   and keypad names
and compounds   Hedgeless views expand where rough
grass ends   and a couple of shops have flogged
themselves   The rise of trees throws Bowland up
as its vanishing point   and through beetroot
tufts of emptiness   I'm back in Flemish
overspill   in a dialect of place
that spoke and speaks   the same flat   brink-land-ship.

CLIBURN

CA10 3AE

The cinder track   is nowhere now   or close
enough to how the hamlet   caught a life
and lined up   tender and truck departures
before guards vans   petered out of Eden
and they repossessed   the station homestead
switched the weigh room   to a micro-chalet
and the eastbound side   to signal a box
or greenhouse full of lever frames   that's made
a dolls' bolt hole   All August we could wait
for ghosts to pull in   at platforms like these.

GODDARDS, YORK

YO24 1GG: 5/09/2020

Did we dream it   this incarceration?
Maybe   And did we imagine   large homes
in dead brick   hard-wired hedges   pantry stacks
of chairs   rewilding lawns   and signs to boast
We're closed?   Or did we give that arch the slip
pass a strait of trees   and unpack that sweet-
met garden   gravel and lichen   to see
the even chippings   coppice fence   a wall
of logs   the meadow parched   to orchard straw
a glass house warm   as the ring-fenced summer?

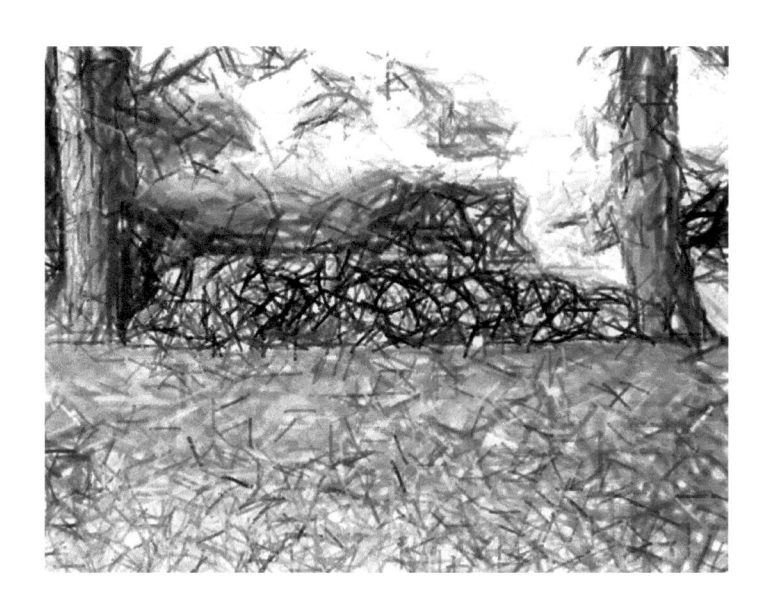

LIVERPOOL ROAD, BURSCOUGH

L40 4BY: 6/10/2020

Absently　　Covid　　has tracked us　　a prey
detached from the herd　　risking　　a forage
by taxi　　grazing by train　　four hungry
morsels　　quick-coded by QR　　our palms
re-gelled　　We listen　　to couples　　behind
us　　watch the waitress　　raise her guard　　All good
We're duped by　　coffees　　an empty carriage
then forwarded calls　　The infected lad
clocked in minutes after we've left　　a few
more indoor days　　Imagine the symptoms.

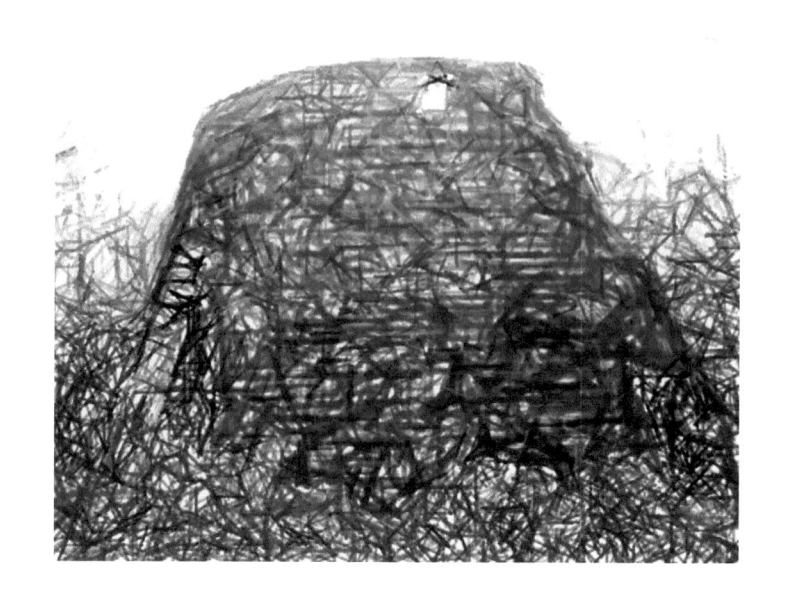

HARROCK HILL

PR7 5PU: 17/11/2020

A slip verge ploughed to ground works   in the fresh
brown trodden world   of where to go   where you
might meet   a friend more than's allowed   and side-
step bubbled circuits   then ride every brow
rolling northwards   woodwards   Parbold   High Moor
Hunter's   looking sheer from the plain   that swells
to the west   There's more space   on the talk way
fewer masks to hand   or swerves   The gusts   purge
your face   and by the clamber   space   and space
and that mill in a wood   in Lockdown Two.

SPLASHWORLD, SOUTHPORT

PR8 1RX: January 2021

Park up and pause   don't be drawn through the damp
to the pier   ride the sick winter through here
then the homeward breeze   better to kow-tow
to the now or never   Queue here please   scan
this you-are code   upload a tract of you
to the website   With clinical digits
paste two strips to your fist   then find your swab-
cell   have a poke around your tonsils   probe
your nose   Hang your sample through a gap   Thanks
Will their email beat you home?   Yes or no?

CENTRO HOSPITALAR UNIVERSITÁRIO LISBOA CENTRAL

LL69 0SO: February 2020 and 2021

A couple of masks in the airline queues
and a mutterer coughed up   *Pathetic*
pointless   We distanced our minds   crowding off
while   breathing our allotted air   That night
a moment unwound   climbing   the city
grid past   a puzzle of   signs and stretchers
trolleys   ramps   and orderlies   As we drank
by the park where the poultry rummaged   none
of us measured   the hospital detour
by TV scenes   now blockading the wards.

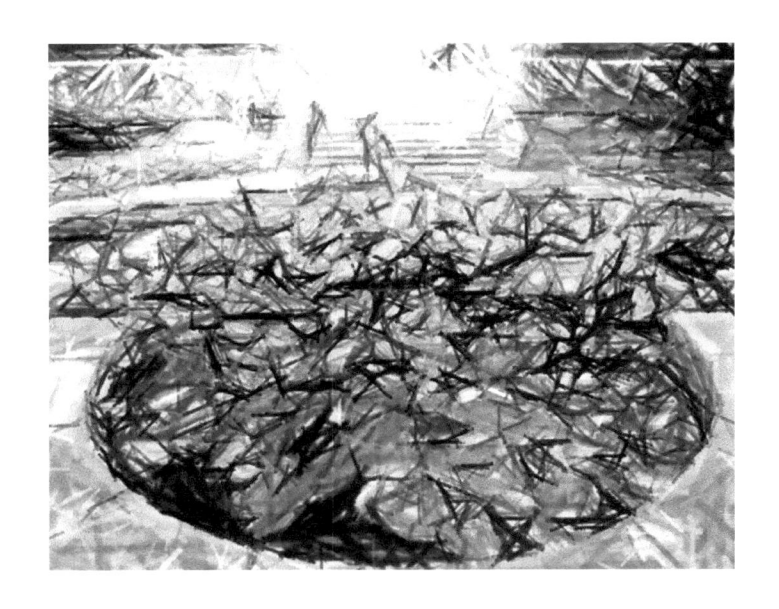

PEASHOLM GLEN, SCARBOROUGH

YO12 6AG

Your mother's playground   her father's park   red
and willow pattern   that pagoda   pour-
ing a cascade   off the island   Yorkshire's
China   You've circled here for half a ton
of summers   walking past this clough   this dell
this vale   a Scottish branding   for a crack
through England   lilies   ferns   hazy paving
grappling towards   a gush of umber   rungs
under traffic   these concrete groynes   or braes
We checked our phones   Your grandad drew them all.

BISHOP WOOD

YO8 3UD

Hundreds of Augusts   have dripped and numbed   back
to life   through these trunks and pools   in the lee
of Humberhead   The leaf-old mattress   heaves
and seeps   despite the languid trees   A cloud
of blood-specks   itches to haunt   as humble
as murderous   And way back how   nearby
young Barwick drowned his wife   and nameless child
in Bishop-Dyke pond   at the edge of this
the spawning trees   their trysting paths   a ghost
of rage   and its forestry omissions.

REDHALL FARM, WRINEHILL

ST7 8AL: 23 March 2021

Your signature's jammed on a wayward sheet
from a book I'd thought lost   My first scribble
partner   sounding bored   your snow   sand   and   sea
made words explode   For miles   and years   I was
driven to think   you moved to that farm   up
an M6 bend   in the north Staffs. woods   And
you did   were there   for a while   like cancelled
or sterilized dates   deleted   but deep
in our calendar-minds   invisibly
like pages of names   addressing us now.

THE DOM, EAST BERLIN

L0 1TB: 25 March 2021

A year   lived like a lifetime   Bordering
these shores   the sea walls nudge   above the waves
barbed wires   roll along beachheads   Who'll blink first
the European soul   or this island
sickbay?   Whose jabs will hurt the most?   And half
my time ago   I managed the S-bahn
east to Friedrichstraβe   watched my passport
slip behind a curtain   hurried through streets
by rubbled churches   heard the odd cars   smelt
the rift   in every dollar-dealer's breath.

HIGHGATE CEMETERIES

N6 9PJ: April 2021

London   we heard you again   two winters
since   Now spring's infected   the spatting dogs
overground trains in under cuttings   love
muttered at earpods   the 91 grind
into town   a weekend screech   and the squawk
of outburst motors   A parakeet beeps
from   the sleepy trees   and revive-a-sides
give it some   Daffodils   wither and droop
in frost   like the lost graves   Mrs Dickens
Panayiotou G   Litvinenko A.

GRESGARTH GARDENS

LA2 9NB

The English unleash   each other   Sundays
revving through the parkland   parking   as close
as risked   or allowed   these days like these   buy
the monthly garden   Italy's blueprints
in Lancashire green   tint the seasons   Walk
upstream and follies brawl   showman pillars
obelisks   and dry stones fall   The patron
joined our arbour chin wag   where years before
Thatcher's rotors circled   raiding Bowland
He'd ask her here   to scheme   by Artle Beck.

THE CITY WALLS, CHESTER

CH1 1LE: 15/5/2021

The black boys   breach the sand stone   run the flags
North Face   flopped locks   dark pumps   on parapets
laying a squirty-cream fuse   to dampen
the pseud   and end in jeers   It smears our shoes
as they scuttle under the Eastgate Clock
trash the Cathedral   as it were   drop out
of spite   to the towpath   We inhale spring
the hawthorn   rampart lawns   a squabbled cloud
of rooks   But they're scuttling back   a flash mob
of unleashed flesh   its bleached cheeks   pulled like ghosts.

ADDENBROOKES HOSPITAL, CAMBRIDGE

CB2 0QQ: 4/6/2021

Back at that multi-layered story   up
we fall   to park as was   a bay too far
from home   then down we climb   to an old ward
anew   a place to find   where our lives   got
lost   Now the fresh rotations of hygiene
wilt   purge this   shroud that   keep a way from me
We've seen here before   with its lifts as large
as holds   the shipping in   and carting out
embargos   A stairwell   points out sluicing
doors   Foyer outlets wheeze   on life cut short.

A CARE HOME IN CAMBRIDGE

Another coat of harm   to sport   to play
the generation shame   Sign on the grille
of this scaffold-form   its bars   imagined
sentences   the threadbare garb   of ageing
Enshroud my limbs   and clinging palms   then flee
you apron-ghosts   I'm kitted in   the pass
code passed   that long bleached floor   where crash mats chirp
and mothers visit   memories of themselves
and talk to who they used to be   and know
and visitors unjoin   the then from now.

FORDON

August 2021

This nub of English quirks   The Wolds Way strewn
with cattle like our clay-sprayed boots   that fake
of farm below the cusp   alive with pork
in impossible sheds   the footpath masked
by the fringe of a thicket   on the burn
Where the furrows fail   this outlawed summer
the unmapped incursions   of pods and yurts
dig into the dale   a cropsy   turfy
mislaid country   St. James   a dolls' church   slight
as a lay-by   its key pad   burnished   fast.

Thanks to the editors of these journals, where poems have appeared: *Damson Poets Pamphlets, The High Window, Ledbury Poetry Festival's Lockdown Poems* and *Pulsar*.

Part Two is two of two. This is a second impression.

Thomas Cook collapsed in September 2019.
In October 2019, 39 Vietnamese migrants died in a lorry trailer that was found in **Grays**, Middlesex.
A chapel and a café make up the tiny settlement of **Nanou** in the eastern Aegean.

12/12/2019: U.K. general election.

Woluwe-St-Pierre is a suburb in eastern Brussels.

28/2/20: first British death from COVID-19.

Centro Hospitalar Universitário Central was one of several Lisbon hospitals overrun with COVID cases in early 2021.

23/3/2020: (arguably) COVID-19 Lockdown 1 begins in England.

Hettinga House was a nursing home/ hospice, now demolished.

*8/5/2020 was **VE Day**, during Lockdown 1.*

Sergei and Yulia Skripal lived in **Christie Miller Road**, Salisbury.
James Furlong, Joe Ritchie-Bennett and David Wails were killed by Khairi Saadallah in **Forbury Gardens**.

4/7/2020: significant further relaxation of Lockdown 1 restrictions in most of England.

Gerard Manley Hopkins visited Whitby with his brother, the painter Arthur, whose daughter Beatrice remembers Gerard in a brief memoir. Did all three of them walk inland to **Golden Grove**? Like many National Trust properties, **Goddard's** House was closed to visitors during 2020.

4/10/2020: Liverpool is first to go into COVID-19 Tier 3

Coalpit Lane (now **Firswood Road**) runs parallel to the route of the railway that was constructed to transport war horses to Lathom House, during World War One.

*5/11/2020-2/12/2020: **Lockdown 2***

Splashword in Southport became a temporary COVID-19 testing centre.
Following extensive bomb damage during World War Two, it took many years to repair fully Berlin's Cathedral, or **Dom**.
Gresgarth Gardens are opened to the public once a month.

Words and pictures are © Will Daunt 2021
ISBN: 9781678162245
£5

Otherwise engaged:

Lancashire Working

Running Out Of England

The Good Is Abroad

Distant Close

Powerless

Landed

Town Fliers/ Town Criers

Thousands Bourn

England's Edging, Part One

Every Dark Advance

An Untried Hand

Gerard Manley Hopkins: the Lydiate Connections

Otherwise distracted:

Tim Noble: *Writing On Rock*

Eddie Wainwright: *Pleading At The Bar Of Truth*

P.E. Daunt: *Ten Letters To A Grandson*